Make Your Own Terrarium

by Rita Alexander

HOUGHTON MIFFLIN

BOSTON

Contents

Background

Terrariums are miniature gardens grown in containers. In some ways, a terrarium is a miniature ecosystem—a community of living things interacting with the nonliving things in their environment.

There are two important differences, however. First, both animals and plants are part of a natural ecosystem. If there are animals in a terrarium, they are usually insects and spiders that are uninvited by the terrarium maker! Second, the terrarium maker—a human—controls all the nonliving parts.

If you make a terrarium, you will need to make sure that the plants you place in it will have all the nonliving things they need to live.

Terrariums can be fancy.

Planning a Terrarium

There are two ways to go about making a terrarium. You can choose plants and then create an environment that will meet the needs of those plants. Or you can create an environment and then choose plants that will do well in it. The plants in your terrarium will need energy, soil, nutrients, water, climate, and air.

Light will provide the energy. Terrariums grow best in clear, uncolored glass because it allows all wavelengths of light to reach the plants. Most terrariums need bright light but not direct sunlight. If you place your terrarium in direct sunlight, you may overheat the tender plants.

Choose a glass container. A plastic container may warp.

The soil in the terrarium will provide nutrients for the plants. It will also contain the amount of water they need. A moist soil generally contains a lot of humus, while a dry desert soil will be about one-third to one-half sand.

An open terrarium can provide a dry or a temperate climate that needs only occasional watering. In contrast, a closed terrarium can provide a moist, or humid, climate.

The shape of the terrarium affects your choice of plants. Some plants need enough room to spread out or to grow tall.

These are types of containers that can be used for large terrariums.

Choosing Plants

The best terrarium plants grow slowly and are small, even when they are full-grown. In addition, they should be suited to the environment inside the terrarium.

For example, if you have a closed terrarium, think about what plants grow well in a humid climate. Ferns and mosses do well in this type of climate. If you want to grow cactus plants, think about the kind of terrarium you need. A dry, open terrarium will create the conditions for cacti. If you want to plant four different kinds of plants, they should need similar amounts of light and humidity.

Here is a list of some common terrarium plants and their water and light requirements.

Desert-Garden Plants		
Plant	**Height (in.)**	**Comments**
Bunny-ears cactus	over 12	Bright light
Haworthia	1 to 6	Medium to bright light
Hen and chicks	1 to 3	Bright light
Jade plant	over 6	Bright light

Insect-Eating Plants		
Plant	**Height (in.)**	**Comments**
Butterwort	1 to 2	Medium light, high humidity
Pitcher plant	6 to 12	Medium light, medium humidity
Sundew	1 to 3	Bright light, high humidity
Venus fly trap	1 to 3	Bright light, high humidity

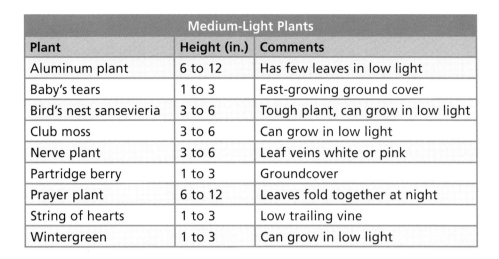

Medium-Light Plants		
Plant	**Height (in.)**	**Comments**
Aluminum plant	6 to 12	Has few leaves in low light
Baby's tears	1 to 3	Fast-growing ground cover
Bird's nest sansevieria	3 to 6	Tough plant, can grow in low light
Club moss	3 to 6	Can grow in low light
Nerve plant	3 to 6	Leaf veins white or pink
Partridge berry	1 to 3	Groundcover
Prayer plant	6 to 12	Leaves fold together at night
String of hearts	1 to 3	Low trailing vine
Wintergreen	1 to 3	Can grow in low light

Bright-Light Plants		
Plant	**Height (in.)**	**Comments**
Joseph's coat	over 12	Keep trimmed
Devil's ivy	over 12	Multicolored leaves
Miniature sweet flag	6 to 12	Grasslike leaves with stripes
Oxalis	3 to 6	Leaves like clover
Moss sandwort	1 to 3	Needs to drain well

Think about the different plants you've seen outside. Some plants can grow in the shade. Others need a lot of sunlight. You will want to place your terrarium where it can be enjoyed but also will receive the light its plants need. Usually the brightest light comes through windows facing south or west. Windows facing east provide medium light, and north-facing windows provide low light.

Planting a Terrarium

When you are ready to begin, gather your materials together. Cover the area with newspaper.

Start by making layers of different materials. Like the layers of soil in a natural ecosystem, the terrarium's layers will allow water to drain, provide nutrients, and help anchor plants.

First, pour about a half-inch layer of small gravel in the bottom of the container. This layer allows water to drain so that the soil does not stay wet. Wet soil leads to root rot and plant death.

Second, spread activated charcoal over the gravel. This special kind of charcoal absorbs odors. It also returns some nutrients to the soil.

Layer gravel, charcoal, moss, and soil in your container.

This is an example of a completed woodland terrarium.

Third, place a thin layer of sphagnum moss over the charcoal layer. The moss stops soil from seeping downward into the gravel layer.

Finally, place a layer of soil over the moss. The soil layer should be at least two inches deep.

Now add your plants. Push some soil aside to make a valley and place a plant in it. Gently replace the soil, making sure the roots of each plant are covered. Do not crowd plants; leave room for them to grow.

Decorate your terrarium with small hills, rocks, moss, or twigs. These will help your terrarium look like a real miniature ecosystem. Then use a spray bottle to make it rain in your terrarium and gently water the plants.

Caring for a Terrarium

You should not have to spend much time caring for your terrarium. A closed terrarium will be humid, like a tropical ecosystem. It will need very little watering because the water is recycled, just as it is in a natural ecosystem.

Water moves up the plant from the plants' roots. Water that isn't used for photosynthesis escapes from the leaves. It evaporates, rises, cools, and then condenses on the sides of the container. Eventually the water droplets slide down to the soil and plant roots. At night, the roots take up water so that the plant can replace water it lost during the day.

An open terrarium can have conditions similar to a temperate climate. It may need to be watered when the soil feels dry. Open terrariums can also be dry like deserts.

These plants need about the same amount of light and water.

Plants can be kept small by cutting back the tips.

The nutrients in the potting soil should be enough to keep plants growing at a steady rate without adding fertilizer. If plant growth slows, gently remove some of the top layer of soil. Then sprinkle new potting soil throughout the terrarium. The new soil will add nutrients for the plants and give your terrarium a fresh, new look.

Although your terrarium may not need a lot of care, it will need regular attention. At least once a week, closely inspect the leaves and stems of the plants, looking for any signs of distress. The sooner you find a problem, the easier it will be to take care of it. Promptly remove any diseased plant.

Troubleshooting Problems

A few weeks after you have set up your terrarium, you may find that some of the plants are not as strong and green as they once were. Here are some common terrarium problems, as well as their solutions.

Sides of container fog with moisture. The terrarium is too moist or too hot. Removing the cover for a day or two should remove excess moisture. Check that the terrarium does not get direct sunlight.

Leaves have brown, dry edges. This may be a symptom of too much heat. Check that your terrarium is not near a heat source, in direct sunlight, or too close to a light. Another cause of this problem is low humidity. Spray a light mist into the terrarium for a few days. Check to see if newer leaves have green, full edges.

Peperomia (left) and nerve plant (right) are two plants that do well in a terrarium.

Lower leaves turn yellow and fall. This can be caused by overwatering, which leads to root damage, or by underwatering, which does not provide enough water to support all of the plant's needs.

New leaves are small and pale; entire plant is spindly. Generally, plants become spindly when there is too little light or they get too little water.

Entire plant droops, looks tired. Droopy plants often suffer from crown, stem, or root rot—all caused by overwatering. Check to see if soil seems too moist or wet.

If you find a plant problem, write down when you noticed it, what you decided the problem might be, and what action you took. These notes will not only help you keep this terrarium healthy, but they will also provide useful information for the care of your next terrarium.

An aluminum plant (left) and club moss (right) are other common terrarium plants.

 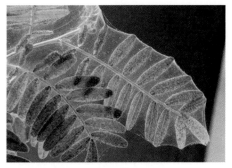

Typical problems may include a plant with aphids (left), or a plant with spider mites (right).

Occasionally you may find that a pest has invaded your terrarium. Perhaps a plant had insects when you brought it home. Pests may also have come from a nearby houseplant. Use the following descriptions to tell what may be affecting your plants and what action to take.

New leaves look small and distorted and have sticky spots. Check the underside of leaves and any new growth for clusters of aphids. Clean any affected areas using a cotton swab wet with a mixture of water and liquid soap.

Tiny white spots appear on leaves. Using a magnifying glass, check for spider mites. Clean undersides of leaves with soap and water. Mites are difficult to control. It may be best to remove the plant from the terrarium before mites move to other plants.

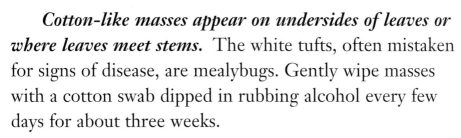

Cotton-like masses appear on undersides of leaves or where leaves meet stems. The white tufts, often mistaken for signs of disease, are mealybugs. Gently wipe masses with a cotton swab dipped in rubbing alcohol every few days for about three weeks.

Small brown oval bumps appear on leaves or stems. The brown bumps are evidence of scale, an insect protected by its shell. Control is difficult, but small numbers of scale can be removed using a cotton swab dipped in rubbing alcohol.

Small white specks appear on plants. White spots usually indicate white fly. These tiny insects will usually fly away at the smallest movement of the plant. As they fly, they look like a small cloud of white dust. Gently clean plants with soapy water.

Other problems include a plant with mealybugs (left), or a plant with scale (right).

Sample Materials List (5-gallon rectangular aquarium)

About 1 pound clean gravel	Aquarium gravel is cleanest and least likely to cause problems.
Small bag potting soil	Do not use soil from a garden. Potting soil has the nutrients your plants need to grow, and it is sterilized to be free from any diseases or pests.
Small package activated charcoal	This is not the same as charcoal used for barbecues.
Small bag coarse sand	Use builders', garden, or sandbox sand. Do not use beach sand.
One small package spaghnum moss	A little spaghnum moss goes a long way.
4 plants, 3-inch pots	One each of miniature peperomia, nerve plant, aluminum plant, and club moss.